Exploring the OpenAI Playground: Unleashing Creativity with AI.

Exploring the OpenAI Playground: Unleashing Creativity with AI.

By: Aaron Cockman
Series: "Smarter Strategies for Modern Business"
Version 1.1 ~March 2025
Published by Sherry Lee at KDP

Table of Contents.

Exploring the OpenAI Playground: Unleashing Creativity with AI. 0

INTRODUCTION..5

CHAPTER 1: OVERVIEW OF THE OPENAI PLAYGROUND. 9

A. OpenAI Playground features.................................10

B. Openai Account And Accessing The Playground. 13

CHAPTER 2: OPENAI MODELS (E.G., GPT-3, GPT-4, CODEX) 18

a. GPT-3: The Creative Powerhouse. 18

b. GPT-4: The Sophistication Continues. 20

c. Codex: The Coding expert. 21

Selecting the Right Model For You. 23

CHAPTER 3: HOW TO EXPERIMENT WITH MODELS IN THE PLAYGROUND. 28

CHAPTER 4: CUSTOMIZING YOUR EXPERIENCE WITH PROMPT ENGINEERING. 34

Key Elements of a Good Prompt. 35

CHAPTER 5: PARAMETERS THAT INFLUENCE OUTPUT (TEMPERATURE, MAX TOKENS, ETC.) 40

CHAPTER 6: CREATING CUSTOM PROMPTS FOR SPECIFIC RESULTS. 46

CHAPTER 7: GPT-3 AND GPT-4 IN THE ART OF TEXT GENERATION..52

CHAPTER 8: BUILDING A CHATBOT WITH CONVERSATIONAL AI. 58

CHAPTER 9: GENERATING CREATIVE WRITING FROM SHORT STORIES TO POEMS...65

CHAPTER 10: WRITING AND TESTING CODE WITH GPT-3/4 IN THE PLAYGROUND. 71

CHAPTER 11: CONTROLLING RESPONSES WITH MODIFIERS AND EXAMPLES. 77

CHAPTER 12: INTEGRATING GPT-3/4 WITH YOUR EXISTING CODEBASES AND REAL-WORLD APPLICATIONS. 84

CHAPTER 13: CREATE YOUR FIRST AI APP WITH OPENAI'S MODELS. 93

CONCLUSION. 102

INTRODUCTION.

Artificial Intelligence has been one of the fastest gadgets to disrupt this world of technology. Over time, a few other innovations have had this speed and thumping genuine buzz. The future that seemed like science fiction before is within reach to redefine how we think, create, and navigate our world.

Coming to AI, one of the guerilla-armed leaders in AI research and development, OpenAI has democratized the supercomputing power of artificial intelligence so much that you can harness its inaccessibly smashing might using simply a pc.

So, how do you even start to dip your toes in the waters of this frontier tech?

How do you progress the GPT-3 and GPT-4 without becoming a raving lunatic of complexity?

That's precisely where I will help you with this book: Exploring the OpenAI Playground.

The OpenAI Playground is an interactive space where anybody, whether you are a developer, artist, writer, entrepreneur, or simply an AI enthusiast, can play around with new models from OpenAI. In essence, it is a sandbox where you can experiment with ideas, adjust the response of AI as laid out in front of you, and make awesomeness, all on the fly. No technical expertise is needed.

The Playground is a home to everyone; whether you're looking to produce some fresh writing, take your automation up a notch, or get technical with code generation, the Playground is for you. But plummeting into the abyss of OpenAI is overwhelming. When tools are abundant in depth and breadth, you ask yourself, what do I do next at OpenAI? And that is why this book exists.

We will explore the OpenAI Playground and reveal how to unlock its full potential with fun and accessible tutorials. Don't worry; this is your hands-on adventurist guide, not a boring technical manual.

For all those attempting to build a chatbot, throw together an AI application, or marvel at how cool the prospects are down the machine learning rabbit hole of horror in Exploring OpenAI Playground, you will be my faithful companion along the way.

This book's heart is an experience about waffling with OpenAI models and discovering how open and sophisticated they are. You will see that soon enough; there are endless possibilities. You can build an AI to write a poem, product descriptions, or anything related to complex decision-making.

Do you want to Develop AI as an assistant for your web or mobile application? It's there for the taking. As beginners in this Playground, we will help you step directly into the AI world without a technical background.

In this book, we will walk through everything you need to know about interfacing with OpenAI's models, from learning the text basics to entering more complex techniques such as prompt crafting and code generation.

We will discuss how to tune AI responses to your taste, what settings and parameters you should try, and how to make AI applications that matter with their colossal functionality. But this book will not end there; we will also inspire you to imagine what AI will do next and ensure you get a view of what lies on the horizon, the next wave of innovations.

The OpenAI Playground is a universe of possibilities. Whether you are a newbie curious, a developer wanting to learn more, or an entrepreneur who wants to run AI for your business needs, the Playground offers infinite opportunities.

You can expect a good grasp of how to experiment with AI streams, fine-tune them to fit your needs, and strive towards what seems impossible at the end of this book. You will leave feeling powerful, having played with bleeding-edge technology that is fun, satisfying, and much more accessible.

So what are you doing? OpenAI Playground is just a couple of clicks away. With our first experiment, we go to the infinite horizon of Artificial Intelligence.

CHAPTER 1: OVERVIEW OF THE OPENAI PLAYGROUND.

The OpenAI Playground is your best friend. It is an easy-to-use, powerful platform that enables amateurs and professionals alike to play around with OpenAI's cutting-edge AI models (GPT-3 and 4, which are my current favorites).

It is a sandbox where you can test AI live like a human. You can ask and manipulate artificial intelligence in real-time to build responses, generate text, or make custom applications without coding. It is a place meant to inspire creative and innovative ideas.

Whether you are a student, an entrepreneur, a developer, or even a layperson interested in AI, Playground gives you everything you need to play and reveal the true AI model's power. You could write poetry and even essays, create conversational chatbots or code solutions in just a few clicks. Let's explore its features below:

A. OpenAI Playground features.

1. User-Friendly Interface.

OpenAI Playground is built for the common person. The layout is straightforward, and the flow of information is simple, leading to a user experience that is one of the most accessible for both newbies and gurus. On Playground, you get a text field with examples of what can be inputted and the AI-generated responses in almost real-time.

2. Various Ai Models.

One of the most impressive things about the Playground is the various GPT-3 and GPT-4 OpenAI models it lets you access. Different models have different strengths.

For example, GPT-3 is very good at writing text that sounds human, and GPT-4 gives you responses that are close to the actual truth and nuance. You can switch between experiment and models with whichever works best for your end goal, whether creative technical debugging, copywriting, or programming an AI assistant.

3. Customizable Parameters.

OpenAI Playground allows you to toggle AI behavior with customizable parameters. For instance, you can adjust the temperature for a more creative or result-oriented AI.

Tunes control the length of the response from the AI; max tokens and top p/frequency penalty will also be used with output diversity and repetitiveness. Using these parameters allows you to configure the output of AI to become your language, for instance, casual chitchat, formal write-ups or very rigid code.

4. Prompt Engineering.

This is where Prompt Engineering comes in, one of the important things in the Playground. Good prompts give you great responses; the better your prompts typically = your higher reaction. You can try different ways of wording your requests and see how the output of the model changes.

A book summary might get you something different than a "brief overview." You can also unlock more accurate and related AI outputs with better prompts for tasks, from anything to technical details, taking you to the recommendation of writing full-fledged code.

5. Interactive Coding and Development.

Within the Playground is an integrated OpenAi's Codex model, so you can write and try code, such as programming direct languages such as Python and JavaScript, in this case. This feature is useful for those who want to create an AI application or to automate things. You can ask an AI for code snippets, debug an AI, and even generate full programs.

6. Real-Time Collaboration.

The Playground is a great collaboration tool; it allows you to share your sessions with others. This is used in the Playground's real-time collaboration feature when you brainstorm ideas with a group, build a project with a buddy or share your results with the digital world; you make it seamless and give each other feedback.

7. Documentation & Support access.

The playground also gives a handout to those who are curious. If you are the type to go off on your own and get into the technical side, you have OpenAI documentation.

This features useful guides, tutorials and how-to's on how to get the most out of the platform. Since OpenAI also has an engaged community around support, it can help with troubleshooting or taking things further.

B. Openai Account And Accessing The Playground.

Setting up an openai account and accessing the playground isn't as tough as imagined. No matter whether you're an old tch geek, or a beginner in AI, follow this steps and in no time, you will be playing with OpenAI's powerful models.

Step 1: To create your OpenAI Account.

Now, the first step that you have to do is to go to the OpenAI website.

1. Visit OpenAI Web Page: type openai.com on your browser and hit Enter

2. Sign Up → The first step on the home page is to click on a sign-up box. Type 'Sign Up' to enter your existing account; if you have one, log in with logged-in credentials.

3. Enter the required information: Name, Email Address, and Password. Choose a strong password for security purposes.

3. Email Verification: You will receive an email after completing the OpenAI form. Go to inbox and click the verification link to verify your account.

Okay! You have an OpenAI account and can play with Playground now.

Step 2: Accessing The Playground.

After your account is created and you're logged in, finding the OpenAI Playground is a breeze. Follow these steps to open Playground and start playing around:

1. Login: If you are not already logged in at openai.com, log in again with your brand-new account and credentials.

2. Go to Playground: From here, there is a link to the Playground in your top menu after logging in. It is often called a Playground. Click it, and you will be landed on Playground's Dashboard.

3. Learn the Interface: The playground is the fascinating part of everything. There is a big text box in the middle. Here, you enter your prompts. At the top is a full menu to tune settings and change the model.

Step 3: Understanding Your Dashboard.

Upon first landing in the Playground, you face an uncluttered and simple dashboard. Let us quickly see the parts we need to cover:

1. Prompt Box: It is the space for Artificial Intelligence to read your guidance. You can tell it to create a story for you, answer the questions, generate the code, etc., or do anything you want to test.

2. Model Selection: Just below the prompt box, you will have the option to select which OpenAI model (e.g., GPT-3, GPT-4) to use. You can use both models for fun, take tasks, and discover how they respond to differing levels of sophistication.

3. Parameters: Facing the prompt box at right, you will find temperature parameters, max tokens and more (changeable). These settings give the AI you're using the room to wiggle and quickly make it more (or less) flavorful/succinct / task-oriented if needed.

4. Playground has examples and templates: You won't need to know what to do if you get stuck or want some examples. Those are great for new people or to steal inspiration.

Step 4: Customizing Your Experience.

In the playground, one of the coolest things about hero-system AI is to customize the outputs generated by the AI. We will go through some settings where you can customize your interactions to best fit with what you need:

• Temperature: This is how much AI would deviate from the straight path because it would make the AI more creative/less predictable. A low temperature (e.g., 0.2) produces a more straightforward and deterministic response, while a high (e.g., 0.8) one results in a relativistic unpredictable solution.

• Tokens: How machines can go on in the response of AI. You can tune this to lower a bit if you just want a short answer, but if you want an explanation, increase the number of tokens.

• Top-up and Frequency Penalty: This helps tweak your responses for a better mix of diversity and relevance.

Step 5: exploring, learning and experimenting

Your account is set up, and the playground is live, so get in! One of the best things about OpenAI Playground is that it is baked to let you try things out. Just start typing your prompts, tweak settings, and allow yourself to get creative. If you get stuck, there are many resources and templates to help you.

You should have gotten all that set up in your OpenAI account and have access to the Playground by now.

CHAPTER 2: OPENAI MODELS (E.G., GPT-3, GPT-4, CODEX)

OpenAI has created a family of models, each good for different things. If you are smart, the Playground can help you get the most out of your data. If you're into creative writing, solving technical problems, or Generating code, several models can help you improve. We will explore the three main models: GPT-3, GPT-4, and Codex.

a. GPT-3: The Creative Powerhouse.

Generative Pre-trained Transformer 3 (GPT-3) is one of the most famous and common models used by OpenAI. It is trained on a collection of books, websites, and other public-access text.

With its large training data, GPT-3 can make astonishingly good general text for almost any task, instead of however dull or convoluted you are.

GPT-3 Key Features:

• Text Generation: Perfection for creative writing, content generating, and Idea brainstorming. If you need to write an essay or compose a sonnet or concept for another enterprise, GPT-3 is there!

• Conversational AI: it is also fantastic for chatbots since the converse is natural. With this model, you can talk about a range of subjects genuinely.

• Flexibility: Having 175 billion parameters (the model's memory) makes GPT-3 able to shift its output to accommodate multiple tones, styles or instructions. It can be used for formal tasks and writing in a non-serious way in a live style.

GPT-3 is amazing but can have flaws. It may sometimes come out with results that ring a little repetitive or misunderstand a very niche topic (though fortunately not to the point of being distinctive). That's where GPT-4 steps in.

b. GPT-4: The Sophistication Continues.

In addition to what GPT-3 can do, GPT-4 further enhances and builds general understanding. Unlike GPT-3 (175 billion parameters), GPT-4 is an even heavier model, which makes it more dependable and generic for harder tasks.

Highlights of GPT-4.

• Better Comprehension: GPT-4 knows many more sophisticated topics and Explicit Instructions in-depth. It is far better at context over longer chats or multi-step tasks and is a clear winner in applications requiring real-depth understanding.

* Correct and Relatable: It will commit fewer errors and give more appropriate replies, especially about specific areas, domains, or controversial discussions. GPT-4 is more right than you to the extent that it follows a discussion better, whether we discuss ancient science or philosophy.

• Increased originality: GPT-4 also integrates with creative work such as storytelling, poems, and technical content. It has sophisticated reasoning capabilities such that it can be more creative with more varied outputs.

The added level of sophistication just translates to GPT-4 being the tool of choice when needing more accuracy or highly specific knowledge. The same accuracy and, more importantly, precision are useful for business applications, educational content, professional writing, etc.

c. Codex: The Coding expert.

We are talking with GPTs in general language models...GPT-3 and GPT-4. The company also created a Codex model for programming-related language models this time. You can complete tasks that involve some coding.

Based on the architecture of GPT-3, Codex is cleverly programmed to comprehend and code in different programming languages.

Key Features of Codex:

• Code Generation: You can ask Codex to generate code snippets, functions or whole applications from a natural language. If you want to make a web app or a Python script or automate something with the help of an automation tool, go on instructions from the brain to the codebase because there is Codex.

• Multi-Language Support: Codex is coded by a person who can read or write code in many programming languages (Python, JS, Java, Ruby/and others) respectively. This makes it super polyglot for developers that work on two or more different platforms.

• Code debugging: Codex can help us in analyzing. It will tell you where it goes wrong, even if the code is broken or you just want to know if your input can produce what output you want with some error messages. It can be a big time saver for developers, especially when debugging complex things.

Codex is mind-blowing, but it is the ideal use case for people who already know some coding. It can make the development process more efficient, though humans might still be necessary to validate that the code is doing what it should.

Selecting the Right Model For You.

Using OpenAI's models for the first time, one can easily not know which to use for every task. Just chill out! Knowing the merits and demerits of the models will lead you to an easy decision-making process and help you get these results within no time. So, how do you select the model that applies to your task?

1. Creative Writing and Content Generation: Go for GPT-3 or GPT-4.

If your task is to write text, be it a blog post, prose or social media caption, GPT-3 and especially GPT-4 are the way to go. These models are fed a huge amount of text and are excellent at making human-like language.

If you want to write broad-form content [GPT-3], you can use it to generate concepts, create blog posts, and even create thought-fuelling dialogue for a script. GPT-3: Excellent for anything beyond heavy technical details or deep understanding.

GPT -4 for more detail/complexity if needed. This is very good when writing something that does not need much depth and nuance, but even then, I would try to avoid writing everything as low as possible.

Both models will be fine for more creative or fine-grained tasks, such as poetry or storytelling, but GPT-4 is likely to be richer and more varied, making it better suited for complex or high-level writing.

2. Coding and Programming Tasks: Choose Codex

For programming tasks like writing code (if any), debugging, or creating a software model, Codex is the model to go for. Codex (Model dedicated to programming and trained to understand natural language about programming metaphors; can be used for code generation)

• Code Generation: Codex is amazing at taking a low-fidelity concept and writing it out completely into working code. Ask Codex to create any function in Python or a web app, and you will receive chunk code in seconds.

• Error Debugging: If you are facing an error in your code, here comes Codex to help. You tell it what your issue is with the bit of code you are stuck on, and Codex will give you fixes to hopefully make you more effective in troubleshooting.

Codex is perfect for the developer, whether you're a complete noob wanting to automate trivial things or an advanced coder hitting a roadblock in your masterpiece. Regardless, wiring Codex has the best results if you know a little programming, as it will make you believe you are a technical person.

3. Handling Complex or Specialized Topics: Use GPT-4.

GPT -4 is the task method requiring deep domain knowledge or complicated data. It improves upon GPT-3 in parsing long chains of complex instructions and can handle rich data points.

• Specialized: GPT-4 can offer accurate and context-aware content on cutting-edge science, medicine, or narrow technical domains, from biotech to cybernetics. It is excellent for educational and research materials or explaining hard concepts simply.

• Consulting and Brainstorming: GPT-4 is one of the best for complex projects and brainstorming ideas. Graph theory is an easy-to-understand mathematical notion but for complex projects. GPT can assist you in designing a multi-step plan, producing major drivers or looking for details of problems that GPT-3 will battle.

For tasks requiring accuracy or precision, especially in professional or academic use cases, GPT-4 is the model. Good when you want to level up the writing (high, medium, technical)

4. Conversational AI and Customer Support: GPT-3 or GPT-4.

GPT-3 and GPT-4 are great with conversational AI, whether for chatbots, customer support assistants, or virtual help desks. Good for GPT-3 when dealing with the average query and easy conversational tasks, but GPT-4 shines on longer conversations or more complex problem-solving.

• GPT-3 works for simple interactions, where the AI has to answer FAQs or point users to relevant documentation. It also works very well in customer support scripts and snappy replies.

• Otherwise, a more nuanced conversation or personalization requires GPT-4 (i.e., AI interprets real-time user inputs, gives nuanced advice, and longer dialog).

5. For Anything In Between: Start with GPT-3 and Experiment.

If in doubt, GPT-3 is a good reference model. It is versatile, easy to use, and can be used across many domains. If you are using GPT-3 to produce text, answer questions or need to automate a process, hey there, buddy, it does it in its mustachioed way.

As you get warmed up with Playground, trial different jobs to see whether GPT-4 is worth your added horsepower or if Codex is a tool for specialized weaponry.

The choice of model for your task comes down to knowing what each model excels at. Content generation is where GPT-3 fits in while GPT-4 is Your Soft Skills Content Science, while Codex is the programming master. By choosing the proper model for your particular use case, you can take advantage of OpenAi's tech stack and do what you set out to conquer the world.

CHAPTER 3: HOW TO EXPERIMENT WITH MODELS IN THE PLAYGROUND.

OpenAI Playground is a wonderful place to mess around and try and tinker with different AI models. As a beginner or at any other level of expertise in the usage, it is quite a delightful and freeing experience to play around with these models and see how much they can do. That's exactly what I'll be walking you through and why it is a fantastic start to unleash the magic of AI.

1. Choose Your Model.

As discussed earlier, your experiment journey begins with deciding which model to play around with later. Playground lets you select from different models, e.g., GPT-3, GPT-4, and Codex, all in one place. Each one has its features, for that you have to choose the task:

• GPT-3: Ideal for creative writing, general text generation and casual conversations

• GPT-4 for tasks that need more specificity and conceptual clarity – the higher order stuff such as technical write-ups or instructions

• LLM (Codex) comes into the picture again as it generates code that is perfect for any programming stuff.

Now that you have picked your model let us get going and allow it to do its thing!

2. Set Your Parameters.

After that, you will customize your ordeal by going through the parameters. This adjusts the parameters until you control how the model behaves, which is important to get what you want.

• Temperature: This tuning influences the creativity and random responses that the model itself will give me. Increasing the temperature (0.8 to 1) makes the model answers more out-of-the-box and crazy. Reducing it further (closer to 0) causes the model responses to narrow and become more deterministic.

Experiment with this to notice a model shift in its tone and creativity.

• Max Tokens: The max response length the model will spit out. Adjust this setting up if you want a longer and more detailed response. It can be lower if you want a short, clear answer.

• Top P (nucleus sampling) – controls the diversity of the answer by restricting the possible answers issued. That is, a value higher (e.g., 0.9) gives the model more options to choose from and yields a more varied response, whereas a lower number makes it opt for the most probable next word from the context.

Play around with these settings to see how the model churns out answers and see if you can get it closer to what suits your use case.

3. Try Different Prompts.

One of the most fun ways to experience what a model is capable of is by playing around with prompts. A prompt is just pasting the information that you are going to feed to the model so it can give you a response. When your prompt is more specific and detailed, the output will be more targeted and accurate. Begin with a simple problem and then make it hard.

• Easy Prompts: Begin asking model easy questions like "What is the capital of France?" or "Tell me a joke." This will help you understand how the model flows out answers.

• Creative Prompts: Write more creative Prompts, like "Capture a dragon baking story." Make it write an outlandish marketing slogan for a new eco-friendly product. The model is unbelievably creative in generating ideas and expressing that creativity!!!

• Technical Examples: If you use Codex or GPT-4, you can also test with technical prompts. E.g., Write a Python script to sort that list of numbers," or "Give me a simple possible definition for quantum physics.

The model will spit text comparable in terms of difficulty to your prompt. The more you play with the different prompts, the more you will learn how and what to use for your use case.

4. Review and Adjust Responses.

After generating the response, review how well the model did. Okay, okay. The response was what you wanted. Was it unique or sufficient graphically/number-wise?

Don't be afraid to rework your query or tweak the rest of it if the answer is not quite right. You may need to elaborate on the instructions, furnish more information, or change settings in model architecture for a more accurate or creative response.

5. Enhance Your Control with System Messages.

You can use system messages (OpenAI Playground) to instruct the AI on how to behave. These are the commands. You give the model these commands before it starts to generate any response.

For example, you could prescript the tone of the conversation and funnel everything down to a single formal response or order a model to act as some character. System messages can steer you in the right direction to get whatever type of response you need, whether that means being serious, laid-back or funny.

6. Save and Share Your Experiments.

As you try things out, remember to save constantly! The Playground allows you to create and save your experiments and share them with other users. This is especially useful when you plan to have a look at your experiments later or show your results to friends or colleagues.

The Playground is a good empowerment tool that lets you play with what AI can do in a simple, transparent, and fun manner. Whether you're just playing around for fun, figuring out how to write a better prompt, or doing more complicated cook-ups, you can get creative and see how OpenAI's models work in multiple ways.

You will learn to play with the different prompts, fine-tune everything by tweaking and exploring the models in between in a range, and then slowly start engaging and getting familiar and comfortable playing with the enormous potential of AI.

CHAPTER 4: CUSTOMIZING YOUR EXPERIENCE WITH PROMPT ENGINEERING.

Prompt engineering has become essential when using OpenAI models such as Hugging Face Transformers (GPT-3, GPT-4). In a nutshell, a prompt is the key to unlocking AI's full power.

If you want to be writing content, answering questions, or programming, getting the prompt is half the battle regarding how far these things will take you. This chapter will break down the basics to get started.

What is Prompt Engineering?

At its simplest, prompt engineering is creating inputs (prompts) on which the AI works as if to yield the best possible outputs. This boils down to knowing how to interact with the model, how one asks such questions, and what to give context to so that the model can answer what we need. The better your prompt, the more precise the amount of relevant and useful answers the AI will provide.

Why is it Important?

Open AI models are highly potent but do not know unless you show them via your commands. With a poor prompt, you may see vague and unhelpful or incorrect answers from the model. Prompt engineering to temper how you engage with the model to get the desired results.

By practicing prompt engineering, you are going to:

• Become more targeted, precise and better Answers

• Saving time by fewer "follow-ups" required

• Boosting the creative capacity of AI for things such as writing, brainstorming, or idea production.

Key Elements of a Good Prompt.

Remember a few things when writing your prompt if you want the language model to deliver the best results.

1. Outline It: What exactly is it you desire? Outline undefined vague prompts such as "Tell me something interesting." This result, generally, answers you can encounter by specifying your desires: "Discuss an interesting fact about space exploration."

2. Context: Supply the context to enable the model to know how it is expected. So, when you are asking the model to write a story, it will be much better if you tell it the genre or some characters in mind, like "Craft me an exciting story based on astronauts and planets". For example, You could say things like, "Create a 30-second sci-fi story long about a young astronaut who finds a new planet

3. Prototype: Explicitly instruct the model of your desired output. If, for instance, you require a list of ideas, ask for that in list format: "Write out five ways to push awareness for my new app." Explicitly stating your required format ensures the model persists and results in your desired format.

4. Tone and Style: Just say what you want, e.g., formal or informal, or even specify the type of tone (the response should be informal but funny, etc.). A slight

tweak like "Write this in casual writing style" or "Provide this formally." might be essential

5. Constraints: Other times, you might prefer your model to behave according to a few constraints. You can say, e.g., word limit or ask for a summarizing: "Key points in 100 words or less" or "in 3 sentences."

Examples of Good and Bad Prompts

To demonstrate a simple notion of what good prompts look like in contrast to not-so-good ones:

Example 1:

Bad Prompt: "Tell me about history."

It is too vague and may answer with a very general response.

Good Prompt: "Compose a 150-word brief outline of the American Civil War

That's explicit and defined with an outline of the length vs. topic

Another example:

• Bad Prompt: "Generate a poem."

It is missing a target & will probably be a generic, unfocused poem.

• Good Prompt: Write a rhyming poem on the theme of nature's beauty with forest and river

Now, the model knows what area, type, and elements are needed for the tailor-fit response.

Experiment and Refine.

What I love about prompt engineering is that it is a learn-through-error process. The more you mess around with unique prompts, the more you will understand what the model likes/does not like with different instructions. Don't be timid in cleaning up your prompts, changing the delivery, or elaborating further. The model didn't give you what you needed, so change your prompt and go from there.

Tips for refining.

1. "ROLE" Prompts: Ask the model to play a role, which will be output in a conversational style. For example, "You are a personal trainer. i.e., create a workout plan for a beginner.

2. Chain of thought: When the model needs to think in steps, use a hinting prompt to ask it to reason it through (e.g., "How do you solve a math problem—one step at a time."

3. Use multiple prompts: You might need a series of prompts for the more complex tasks. You can add follow-up questions that expand on earlier responses and lead to a better answer by building on what has been said.

Prompt engineering is a brilliant tool to utilize, so you can leverage the strength of OpenAI Models. Prompt engineering throws a door to a universe of creativity, problem-solving or automation that you can unlock with concise yet meaningful & context-ridden prompts. You should try your prompts differently, see the results, and give the AI a chain to do the same things you do.

CHAPTER 5: PARAMETERS THAT INFLUENCE OUTPUT (TEMPERATURE, MAX TOKENS, ETC.)

When using OpenAI models like GPT-3 or GPT-4, what you receive as outputs is based on your prompt and an outcome heavily influenced by some of the following key parameters: the outputs.

The temperature and max tokens (top_p, etc.) are just among all the other parameters that influence how this model (or any past or present state-out-GPT) will respond, so they give you knobs on style, creativity and length. Learning these parameters will help you improve your results more aligned with your requirements.

1. Temperature.

The temperature parameters control this model instance response's developmental ability and out-scale. It is between 0. and 1.

• Low temperature (0.0— 0.3): By reducing the temperature, your model is going under determinism mode. It will select the next word with the highest probability in the context. Good at generating factual, accurate or ask-number using tasks, i.e., answering questions and making some content (e.g., hypotheses)

•High Temperature (0.7–1.0): When the temperature is high, the model becomes creative (and less choosy, lowering the unlikeliness of choosing those wonderful, less likely, more semantically diverse responses.). This is handy for making up stories, just throwing out an idea, or when you truly desire a new perspective.

For instance, if you request the product description, a lower temperature would deliver a more direct and professional description. However, for something more creative and fun, a higher temperature would provide something more imaginative.

2. Max Tokens.

Max tokens indicate how many tokens (words, parts of words or punctuation) are allowed for a response from this model. Tokens can be as short as words (e.g., a) or multiple words, e.g., conversation.

• Shorter Max Tokens: The output will be short by limiting max tokens (50 or less). Perfect for: you only want a concise answer or an abstract.

• Higher Max Tokens: The model can build more complex and elaborate responses if you define higher max tokens (500 or more). Used for writing essays, long-form content or expressive explanations.

Remember, the model will stop at the max (prompt + completion) token limit; configure! If you want a long text response, give a suitable limit!

3. Top_p (Nucleus Sampling)

Top_p is a different form to limit diversity in model response. Rather than sampling freely from all possibilities, top_p restricts the selection to the top most likely words but introduces unpredictability nonetheless.

• Low Top_p [0.1–0.3]: With a lower setting for top-p, some of the model focuses only on top probable outcomes, making its responses more predictable, focused, and conservative.

• High Top_p (0.5–1): higher top_p allows for a more diverse and creative response. The model has more options to choose from, thus producing varied outputs.

One of the beauties of top_p is that it works with temperature to dial in how conversational or formulaic you want from responses. For a balanced amount of creativity without going over the top with randomness, top_p is for you

4. Frequency Penalty.

Frequency Penalty: this affects the ease with which the model thinks other words will be repeated in the same response. These parameters can be between 0 and 2.

• Low-Frequency Penalty (0.0 –0.5): The model tends to repeat words, so this setting allows repetition of words, which could be useful if you generate something where repetition works (e.g., Poetic structures or verse in music).

• High Frequency (1.0–2.0) — This parameter will penalize the model from repeating words or phrases. Perfect for when you need variety in the answers, you introduce a slight element of randomness to not freak out all over the output, particularly when longer outputs.

Use a higher frequency penalty to ensure that the model does not reuse a word but rather changes it up a bit with something new when generating writing.

5. Presence Penalty.

Presence penalty: works similarly to the frequency penalty, which urges the model to generate variant words or ideas but instead avoids over-cluttering with repeated topics or topics. It is also from 0 to 2.

• Low Presence Penalty (0.0-0.5): the model will give more results with the initial prompt and will not move forward much.

• High Presence Penalty (1.0–2.0): This setting activates the exploration of new topics and ideas. It's good to use if you want the model to produce more varied content or prevent it from immediately falling into one space.

6. Stop Sequences.

Stop sequences so that you can tell the model to stop producing text. The latter is excellent for responses that want a finite phrase or word to mark the end (i.e., inside dialogue structured content). You can set one (or many) stop sequences to ensure the model doesn't completely derail.

For example, if you were crafting a story, you might write a stop sequence, something like "The End," just in case this story goes on all night.

Once these parameters impact the model's outputs, you can shape your responses to adopt a different mindset. Whether you're creating creative storytelling, brief answers, or technical writing, changing token temperature and top_p parameters can tweak how the AI behaves. Have fun with all these settings and discover what works for you when using OpenAI models. The more you try, the more you will unlock them all.

CHAPTER 6: CREATING CUSTOM PROMPTS FOR SPECIFIC RESULTS.

With OpenAI models such as GPT-3 or GPT-4, the trick to getting the perfect response is mainly injecting your custom prompts.

Custom Prompt Input: A customized input that tells the model to spew out an output in the form that you desire.

Learning how to create custom prompts will exponentially increase the value of the results no matter how you create content (no pun intended), come up with a solution, or need specifics.

With OpenAI, you can respond and customize your text based on WHAT you ask (the power of context and instructions). You can tune your prompts to steer the model to do certain tasks, characterize voices or write in multiple styles or formats. So, this is how you create a custom prompt for your required results.

1. Be clear and concise.

The first step in creating a prompt is defining exactly what you want. Broad prompts = broad results, so be as specific as you need to be or the task/result you are trying to achieve. The way to show a model the exact list of blog post ideas about fitness is quite a simple prompt: "Think fitness blog ideas," but with context, that can get better.

Instead, "Provide 1/10 breakeven unique blog post topic ideas around fitness (beginner-friendly, strength training, healthy eating, etc.)" This is much more explicit and straightforward and gives the model an idea of something more targeted and related.

2. Expectations on Output Format.

One of the other key components of custom prompts is telling the model how you'd like it structured in the response. Whether you are looking for a list of bullet points, a summary or a full-fledged essay, serving that model a little nudge in your direction will seriously improve the results you get right here.

E.g. For a product description, "Create me a 150-word product overview of a sustainable yoga mat (It is made of eco-friendly materials and the feature of durability dynamite. This is precise for the kind (description), the word count (150) and the focus (green, durable-durable).

You can say, "Write a dialogue about their trip plans between two friends. One friend is super pumped, while the other worries about creative writing/dialogue work.

3. Tone | Adjust your Style.

The tone and style of the output are everything. Sometimes, you might wish for a more formal and professional response, and other times, you may want something more casual or humorous. Tuning the tone can be as simple as tossing a few words into your prompt.

You can even tweak the tone with this:

"Compose a professional email to your client with the subject line "Thanks for Purchase" reminder and ask if it needs to be.

• Promotional ClickBait / "Just launched" ice cream flavor: "tweeny yanda twittah"

• Argue a Case for a College Graduate Student.

With a level of tone in mind, whether that should be formal, friendly, funny or motivational, the model can tailor its answer to your requirements.

4. Put in some Suggestions or Constraints.

This leads to constraining the model and eliminating the junk from the result. For example, if you want to prevent your model from repeating certain words from now on to emphasize particular themes or only be constrained in length, then those details give the model an idea of what to focus on.

For instance:

• "Write a 200w op on how daily walking is not an exercise but good enough."

• Develop a 5-step productivity-boosting process, each up to 50 words.

These additional constraints should finally give you the most relevant and targeted output. You may provide further instructions like "use three bullet points" and "write positively."

5. Use Role-based Prompts.

A technique for generating custom prompts is assigning a model to a particular role. This will help the AI think and write like an expert in his/her field should have done. You would ask the model to operate as a "nutritionist" in this scenario or tutor when you need some educational advice and a business consultant otherwise.

Examples:

• (As a professional chef) Create a 30+ under vegetable and vegan dinner recipe for me.

• As a CRM strategist, write down the blueprint for enhancing team collaboration in a virtual environment.

This method aids in producing more courteous and appropriate answers to guarantee that the model delivers what was expected.

6. Refine and Experiment.

We are going to iterate craftily by creating custom prompts. You may not always get what you wanted the first time, and you're not doing something wrong! Once you look at what the model produced, think of improvements to be made. Context? More guidance? Otherwise, it has a different vibe!

For instance, when you request a vague product description, edit your prompt by adding more specific facts about your product.

•Specific features such as who will use this app or comparison with competitors.

After all, each time you try different things, it just makes your model aware of how that model reacts to some input. If you are making up stories, working on problems, or coming up with fresh ideas, custom prompts mean you have control over what output you are getting. Begin rudimentarily, be straight up and improve your prompts over time, and you will start producing what you need faster and better.

CHAPTER 7: GPT-3 AND GPT-4 IN THE ART OF TEXT GENERATION.

At heart, GPT-3 (Generative Pretrained Transformer 3) and, likewise, GPT-4 were (and still are) the original supermodels generated by OpenAI in an amazing series of models.

These specialized models should be able to understand and generate human-like text based on what was fed into them. They do answers questions, write essays, story generation from words to a ball of crap but also have conversations on difficult topics.

1. Scale and Size.

GPT-3 and GPT-4 are such on a large scale. Take, for instance, GPT-3, which has 175 billion parameters—it is probably the biggest AI model that exists. These are the internal configurations that the model learns. At the same time, training and having more of them usually leads to higher patterns in understanding the power of a model and producing more accurate outputs.

GPT-4 then goes a step further and has more parameters on all counts, translating to an even better sense of subtlety and nuance and the ability to handle complex tasks, too. The massive scale, in turn, lets them store more context over a more significant portion of text (10,000 words) and produce elaborate answers that add a layer of sophistication.

One of these scales is why the text is a lesson in feeling natural and organic at these model's levels (at least for what they can do).

2. Contextual Understanding.

Deep in context, unlike earlier AI models, which use keyword matching or just line-by-line pattern recognition with GPT-3, and bloody hell, GPT-4, seriously. So they do not take in only the last words you wrote or the most recent input but ALL CONTEXT OF conversation /prompt. That allows them to give more on-point and connected responses, possibly even for complicated or multi-step tasks.

Let's say you ask GPT-3 and GPT-4 a question requiring them to remember something from earlier in that conversation so they can follow the context and update that knowledge in what they say. The ability to "remember" and use context makes talking with these models feel more fluid than simple search returns, and the difference appears in how they interact.

3. Flexible and Adaptable.

GPT-3 and GPT-4 also do one of the best things: They offer considerable flexibility. These models are good at dialing any task you throw at them without having to train from scratch. They can do much, from writing essays and stories to solving math problems or coding.

How they are trained gives them this flexibility. GPT-3 and GPT-4 are pre-trained on large amounts of text data extracted from the internet, including books, sites, and texts in general.

Their general exposure ensures they can write on almost anything, whether science/art/history/technology, etc., making them very general. They are not trained for each task; they must be fed new input and produce in-phase output.

4. Human-Like Text Generation.

However, the most impressive part of GPT-3 and GPT-4 is how they can produce nearly human-like text. The models are neither mere "spitters" of phrases nor sentences following a specific pattern.

They have relatively advanced knowledge of language flow, cadence, and use. These models can generate responses that favor the tone and style you want to ask for, whether it formally sounds like a business letter, hardly written blog post, or creatively flows a short story.

The model's ownership of the transformer architecture allows them to look ahead a good distance in text. The former can help with even more intricate concepts of words, phrases, and sentences being taught by them. Thus, it leads to text that is not only correct and syntactic but also compelling and relatable.

5. Hyperparameter Tuning and Customization.

GPT-3 and GPT-4 are forcefully intuitive in their general capabilities but also trained generically specific enough that they can be fine-tuned or customized for many things.

For example, suppose you tackle a specific project, such as legal documents or medical writing. In that case, you can fine-tune the model to better resemble the language and vocabulary used in those fields.

With customization allowed, these models are even more powerful, which implies the ease of fulfilling hardcore atomic requirements while still keeping their main essence of general text generation. This flexibility means you can use GPT-3 and GPT-4 for everything from ladder writing help to professional domain-specific tasks.

6. Active learning and iteration.

GPT-3 and GPT-4 can revise their responses based on what they get sequentially from the input. In other words, you can interact back and forth with the model to make better output.

So, the response that came out of the model can be pretty far away from what you wanted — you can rephrase or refine your instruction and the model will re-do its thing. This dynamic and interactive learning enables these models to be enormously handy for users who want to test inputs to see if they overflow or die.

Overall, GPT-3 and GPT-4 are differentiated in scalability, context-understanding power, versatility, and human-like text generation. These models are not just action—they can converse, evolve, and produce quality content across multiple subjects or assignments.

The GPT-3 and the GPT-4 are distinct in their pureness of creativity (along with a counterpart one-time fluency) when it comes to writing automation or solving hard problems you have in mind and making fascinating conversational experiences.

Delving into these models gives you a glimpse of infinite potential on the border between AI and human-like cognition as we explore what can be and expand those limits daily. Automating text generation in GPT-3 and GPT-4 is not the future; rather, it is the evolution of intelligent, interactive systems that feel more like friends than tools.

CHAPTER 8: BUILDING A CHATBOT WITH CONVERSATIONAL AI.

The days of a far-fetched chatbot that can speak with you meaningfully are passé; thanks to large strides in artificial intelligence (AI), it is now feasible and within reach.

Through the cutting edge of artificial intelligence (AI), from building a customer service chatbot to an entertaining conversational partner or a productivity pal, it has never been easier or more accessible to build conversational AI.

So, how do you build a chatbot, and what is required to be convincing (for a few months)?

Take this process one step at a time and the key elements that make an AI chatbot appear conversational and useful.

1. Define Your Chatbot's Goal.

Before delving into technicalities, the fundamental job of a chatbot must be defined. You may have a chatbot to answer customer service queries, some navigational questions for a website, general queries related to something else or just be asked for entertainment!!

It is important to figure out what you hoped the goal would be when you created this, and from there, the CHATBOT Style in tone and language will be determined through the responses it provides.

2. Choose the Right Platform and Tools.

Having defined the purpose, you can now choose the tools and platforms that will make your chatbot come to life. Today, many options prevail, but two fundamental approaches can be observed in the practical world.

Rule Chatbots: These kinds of bots are based on some rules and responses. With a script, they work the best for straightforward, clear-cut interactions. For instance, a bot asking FAQs is rule-based because it will maintain a search for keywords in the user input and give an answer from a database where the answer is loaded.

• GPT-powered Chatbots: AI bots that generate replies using sophisticated GPT-3 or GPT-4 models. Where they do this, they analyze a larger variety of queries and can do so rather than following rigid rules. This is perfect for you when the story needs to be more conversational and can handle complex /highly jumpy conversations.

Dialogflow, Rasa, and Botpress are only a few platforms that allow you to easily connect speech-powered AI chatbots over a website or mobile application and social media. Services like OpenAI's GPT models provide access to excellent NLP, allowing you to develop chatbots with proper humanlike dialog.

3. Designing Conversations and Responses.

To keep your chatbot interesting and unforced, you must work conversationally, such as designing. How a user will pass the bot and what sounds human-like responses should be along with natural gazes.

First Step: List the most common user queries and responses here. A bot should be able to understand the query if a user asks, for instance, "What time are you open?" and respond with the appropriate answer, "We are open Monday to Friday, 9 am-5 pm. What about the complex questions? Does the user get touchy?

AI models, for instance, GPT-3, can interpret and make sense of a user's message intent, giving more context-aware replies. The chatbot is not a hard-coded script and can provide more context-aware answers. You could say, "I am truly sorry to hear you are so upset. So let me help you with that!" Use a bit more one-tone but human and accessible.

4. Train your Chatbot.

Training a chatbot, whether you're using a rule-based or AI-powered solution, is key to a substantial part of the process. For rule-based bots, this means configuring pre-defined responses and making decision trees for every possible conversation path.

Chatbots that use AI need to be trained on large data sets so that the model learns how to respond to different scenarios as is.

It may be difficult, but this process is fundamental for increasing your bot's knowledge and output for few-shot learning of models such as GPT-3 in AI chatbots (e.g., healthcare, tech support, etc.). The bot will be more complex and polished in responding to every data point and interaction in the model.

6. Testing and Iterating.

Building a conversational AI is an iterative process. Once your bot is built, be sure to test it thoroughly. Interact with the bot in a way that allows a user to see if it can respond properly and assist. Ask everything you can get in diversity to find out its limitations and feedback.

Monitor areas where the bot fails in testing, such as misinterpretations, lack of customization, and generic responses.

6. Scaling and Deploying.

After your chatbot has been tested and polished, it's time to deploy it. All platforms have simple integration methods for web, apps, or messaging services like Facebook Messenger, Slack, WhatsApp, etc. Verify the bot's availability live and monitor its progression.

Your chatbot will start getting popular and you will need to scale it to support high QoQ user interactions.

Most AI-powered chatbots can be scaled to deal with large volumes of users without the need to keep reprogramming. So, pay attention to the performance metrics and user satisfaction with which the chatbot is used.

7. Observe and enhance the User Experience.

Monitor conversations to identify hurdles, log recurring problems, and check whether users ask for directions. We can update AI chatbots by learning from their past conversations so that they become smarter and better solutions over time.

For instance, users frequently request a feature that your bot cannot deliver and you would like to add that capability to increase user delight. Further, the chatbot will use machine learning algorithms to grow emotionally and insightfully smart with context.

A chatbot is a perfect first technical challenge (if not a good project to start building with your newly acquired skills), but it can be somewhat daunting initially. If you want to build a chatbot for work or pleasure, the diversity and capabilities of GPT-3 and GPT-4 make creating true conversational AI virtually effortless!

An AI-assisted bot that answers the question, engages the user and adds real value by concentrating on user requirements and constantly training to make the bot flexible. Your chatbot can blossom into a best friend if you only have a little creativity, i.e., you truly chat and feel natural.

CHAPTER 9: GENERATING CREATIVE WRITING FROM SHORT STORIES TO POEMS.

Creative writing is a wide and ever-expanding world where you can create complex stories or say what hearts feel through poems. AI can be used by a pro writer or a newbie to generate ideas to break writer's block or help you compose your draft documentation.

Steps for utilizing AI to help with Writing.

1. Jumpstart Your Creativity.

Writing creatively always begins with the hardest part -creating that initial spark. Well, you may have the topic you want to tackle but the problem is, writing it. AI makes a huge difference here. AI can give you a good opening line, an outline, and a write-up to start your creative process.

If you are writing a short story and you do not know how to, at least you can give your characters to AI by briefly describing them, dialogue, scenes or whole opening sentences to start with, which you can shape; it will get you out of the box in no time and get the creative juices flowing so writing does not appear as an overwhelming task.

2. Write Poetry That Resonates with You.

Writing can be powerful and intimidating all at the same time, especially poetry. The poem's essence is often its rhythm, metaphor, and voice. With its functionalities, AI can help you experiment with different styles, tones and formats to discover what elicits your greatest emotional or thematic response.

AI can generate poetry in many styles, from haikus to free verse and even poets you admire. There is no point for humans. You can tell the AI what theme or a few words you have in mind and it will word lines like someone who can string phrases together.

For example, you could prompt a poem on love, nature or loss and have it spit out verses that sound like a thoughtful poet did.

Imagine you want to find a rhyming couplet of a nice, jolly, warm summer evening. The AI might suggest:

"Solar aureole is sinking slow and soft, Casting shadows where floral fall.

You can always polish and develop these ideas or use them to start your journey to poetry. The limit is the sky and people can use AI to create poetry that has emotions with their creative mind.

3. Storytelling / Fiction Writing.

A great ally for fiction writers is AI, which can help us write a draft of the story by giving us hilarious plot ideas, creating/heroes, and even inventing dialogue. Think about being able to hook up a minimal premise. Maybe you want a detective who solves a mystery in a small town, and AI can feed you a complete outline and even answer your first draft.

Experiment with all the genres: romance, sci-fi, fantasy and even historical fiction, just to see which thoughts are cast. AI, which does world-building? AI can give worlds and places to live in that feel real.

For example, if you are writing your fantasy and looking for a new species of creature in that world you have been creating, you can easily ask for an AI-generated description of a dragon race. It will produce an IP of your creatures' traits, behaviors or backstories.

AI can even write dialogue in the style of characters you characterize, with an understanding of context [1]. This is perfect for kind of Sound In Your Writing of Different Personalities. This is something you can ask AI to come up with a dialogue between two characters like a sage mentor and their excited student and it generates responses according to the personalities you specified.

4. Refining and Tools to Improve Writing.

AI is an amazing instrument for refining and amplifying your creative writing. AI can help you read through and improve your poems or stories once you have written something.

It can automate synonyms along a definition, suggest sentence rewordings or even state improvements in your writing. Sometimes, you need feedback about your writing to see it fresh again. AI objectivity can give you the guidelines to edit your work without bias to make it more complete.

5. Busting Writer's Block.

We all have days where inspiration goes out and writing can dry up. Fortunately, with some help from AI, these travails make better times. If you are in a funk and unsure what to write next, you can [ask] AI to take over your next paragraph, think of ways to resolve your plot and even generate a brand-new idea.

When you need ideas, AI has you covered (fill in the blank: If working on a fantasy novel and need to know what to write next? For example, maybe your protagonist is at an important crossroads and the AI says, "Hero discovers hidden map with secret treasure but trouble as well.

This prompt will now open a new chapter in your writing.

6. Related Writing Prompts and Challenges.

For challenge junkies and inspiration seekers writing, AI can spit out some genre or theme-specific writing prompts. Need help with writing something dystopian post-apocalypse or historical? Just ask the AI to generate a prompt for you. You can also use AI for creative writing exercises: Write like this or the die style of an author and pair two different genres.

You may query AI to feed it a mystery and romance writing prompt. For example, "A detective developed a taste for the suspect in this murder case, but the closer he investigates, possibly nobody they fall in love with is the other side of a piece (twist). This prompt can seep some inspiration into what you need to hop and jump to start your next project.

One of the cool aspects of AI for creative writing is it does not take away your creative role as a human artist. Instead, it broadens your wherewithal unto others' eyes and takes you from a never-ending place to inspiration. If you are penning a novel, composing a poem or brainstorming for novel ideas to present your thoughts, AI offers the tool and freedom to push your creativity to extremes.

It's not about kicking your voice to the curb but enabling you to iterate new thoughts and breakthrough creative stalemates, sending the writing places you never thought possible. Enjoy the possibilities and use AI as your writing coach that unlocks your complete creative power.

CHAPTER 10: WRITING AND TESTING CODE WITH GPT-3/4 IN THE PLAYGROUND.

OpenAI Playground is a wonderful interface that allows you to play with GPT-3 powered models or even GPT-4 and write test code. There is the Playground; no matter whether you are a newbie in programming or a pro who wants to speed up his code creation process, it serves as a simple place where you can generate code and then see it live.

Using GPT-3/4 for Coding.

After you access the Playground for the first time, you will notice a simple interface where you enter text, and the AI will work with you. All you have to do to start writing some code is show GPT-3 or GPT-4, a natural language input containing what you want to accomplish with your programming.

For example, if you would like to create a simple Python Function for an if statement to find a prime number, you can try something like this:

Write a Python function that determines if an input number is prime.

Within seconds, the model spits out some code after you request this. Here's an example of what the output might be,

```python
def is_prime(num):

  if num <= 1

    return False

  for i in range 2, int(num ** 0.5) + 1

    if num % i == 0

      return False

    return True
```

This quick output will help you jump right in without writing everything from scratch.

Playground Testing Code.

Generating code is good, but testing is mandatory to ensure the correctness of the code. While the Playground is great, it lacks a direct code execution environment, so you can't run the code on their platform. In any way, we will use GPT-3/4 to assist you with code that can live test somewhere else.

Mastering GPT-3/4 for testing code.

Step to debugging: if your code and the code is not working, input it into the Playground; GPT-3/4 asks what your intention is when you write a step-by-step help debug using it.

You can offer a prompt like "What is the mistake in this Python code and advice for debugging," which leads you towards helpful corrections. A GPT-3/4 model can inspect the code and provide a hint of what is likely broken so you know common errors.

• Unit Testing: If you need to ensure your code works, ask GPT-3/4 to take the unit tests you've coded.

For instance, suppose you have created a function and then fed such prompt to GPT-3/4: "Now write unit tests for is_prime function in Python."

This can result in the model generating tests like:

```python
import unittest.

class TestPrimeFunction(unittest.TestCase):

 def test_prime(self):

  self.assertTrue(is_prime(5))

  self.assertFalse(is_prime(4))


 def test_edge_cases(self):

  self.assertFalse(is_prime(1))

  self.assertFalse(is_prime(0))


if __name__ == '__main__':

 unittest.main()
```

This ensures your code works with typical cases, stupid uses, and edge conditions.

Optimizing Code for Performance.

When your code is working, you may try to tweak it. GPT-3/4 makes you better at improving performance in your code. For instance, the plain "Optimize this python function for better performance" can churn out courses to make your code more compact, faster or more readable.

Polishing your code.

As you progress with the code, you may use GPT-3/4 again to improve it. Ask for tweaks in the structure and accessibility or to adhere to best practices. You can then make clean and efficient code while rolling out your features and the feedback from the AI.

Iterative Process.

A major advantage of GPT-3 / 4 in the Playground is that it lets you write iterative code. The AI will help you refine your code interactively by trying new solutions and giving fresh insights over and over again. This ultimately means coding faster, better and smarter.

I made a code sample using a text generation tool, and I want to test the generation of new features or change some function behavior. For GPT-3/4, you must change the prompt, and the model will offer an updated code that accounts for your new specs.

Empowering the Developer.

Beginners find the Playground to be an amazing primer for learning. This enables you to play with coding concepts and experience coding. GPT-3/4 will lead you, step-by-step, through to understanding syntax and knowing how to create the most basic structures.

The Playground for the Veterans speeds up your development, as it does all monotonous tasks such as debugging code or making solutions pretty fast. It offers a robust AI assistant capable of everything from churning boilerplate code to simplifying convoluted algorithms.

Whether you are merely starting or are an experienced developer trying to optimize your process, applying GPT-3/4 on Playground embodies the power that truly changes how we code and test our code.

CHAPTER 11: CONTROLLING RESPONSES WITH MODIFIERS AND EXAMPLES.

The more you plunge into OpenAI's Playground, the more you will realize that the platform offers expert settings (hence, you can control the model output). Modifiers: these settings (called modifiers) are awesome; they can tailor the output better in finer ways. They will help you steer the model's answers closer to your specifications in kind (tone), creativity, length, or genre.

In this chapter, we will dive a little deeper into some of the main modifiers and how to use them effectively so you can generate the response styles you desire.

1. Temperature.

One of the Crucial Debuggables is temperature. These tips are for the most important modifier. It changes the degree to which the model responds to randomness or creativity. You use it to tune the answers to be machine-predictable or creative.

• Low Temperature (0.0-0.3): setting this too low will make the model output more focused/deterministic. For easier responses containing no surprises, it is ideally suited for getting simply basic or fact-based.

Low temperature, e.g., asking for a definition of "machine learning," would yield an exact, factual answer.

• High Temperature (0.7 ~ 1.0): This setting will prompt the model to find creative and explore various possible responses. Excellent for creative use cases (whatever writing story, idea generation and varied content).

For instance, As you ask your model to write a plot for a short story at a higher temperature, it will become more varied and even fantastical.

Temperature adjustment is how you refine the balance between creativity and perfection so things will be exactly how you want them for what you aim for.

2. Max Tokens.

Number of tokens the model is allowed to produce with one response. This is the limit of what the model can output (aka how many characters, in as small or large as terms are words)

Short Max Tokens: If you need answers in vain, set the max tokens to fewer. A low token count will result in plain-talking for a quick definition or definition.

If, for example, you are only looking for the definition or summary, a lower max tokens value, e.g., say 1024, will make the response short.

E. For instance, asking for a small "short description of the solar system" will result in a quick (50-100 words) response if the tokens to maximums are set small.

• Long Max Tokens: If you're producing longer forms, like articles, essays or around a detailed description, a higher token limit Long Values.

Example: A "Comprehensive Personal Finance 101" request with the maximum tokens enabled will generate an exhaustive, longer, more detail-oriented response.

The max tokens setting can manage how short or long you think your responses should be, which is useful for toning down the stream of consciousness.

3. Top_p (Nucleus Sampling)

Top_p controls the level of randomness in responses to your model word selection and operates over a constrained set of high probabilistic subsequent candidates.

You get more focused and predicted output when using a lower top_p value because the model will decide from fewer alternatives. A higher top_p allows the model to draw words from a broader selection of possible outputs, which can result in more creative and varied outputs.

• 0.1-0.3 Low top_p: used it to set the model to the most probable words from those available for the response to sound more coherent and less surprising.

It mostly works for more logical or factual types of tasks.

Example: Requiring a scientific talk or technical details with a low top_p would result in a thought-out answer that is clear & cold, hard fact.

• High Top_p (0.7 to 1.0): Top_p = further loosens the narrowing of options and allows the model an increased scope to search for words or ideas. This is super awesome for more creative work (like writing fiction or devising weird solutions to problems)

Example: You ask for a "dragon story" top_p set high; the result will be far outlandish and inspired.

Top_p and temperature give you very good control over how creative or structured the response should be.

4. Frequency Penalty and Presence Penalty.

These two settings will help in limiting the repetition of answers in the model:

• Frequency Penalty: A modifier to decrease the chance that the model simply repeats the same words. The higher, the less the same word or phrase will be used in a sequence (aka penalty).

For example, when writing a poem or free writing and the model gets stuck repeating the same concepts, a frequency penalty increase in the +ve area will push for more diverse language from the model.

• Presence Penalty: The opposite of being too close to a previous topic, this will push the model to bring new things. A larger presence penalty means the model is nudging us more to develop new ideas.

Example: If you tell the model to compose a tale about a trip, the presence penalty suggests that the model reflects the journey differently instead of repeatedly visiting the same locations or ideas.

This helps to keep things fresh and diverse in longer output responses / creative tasks, which are both penalties.

5. Stop Sequences.

Well, stop sequences let you tell the model when to stop spitting out text. This is especially helpful for constraining the form and the output length. You can include one or more stop sequences, e.g., a word, short phrase or punctuation, to indicate that the response has been completed.

-Example: Use" END OF DIALOGUE " at stop sequence any denotes to the model that this is where it should finish generation on this phrase in a dialogue you're writing.

Stop sequences are fantastic for finessing when and where the output should stop so that the output is within your defined spaces.

These settings will be the most useful when using advanced settings and modifiers in Playground on OpenAI. These settings give you exactly what you need to nudge the limits of the good actual answer vs the Creative/imaginative response you want.

Tinker around with temperature, max tokens, top_p and other parameters and marvel at the enhanced responses. The more you play with these advanced settings, the more control you will have in fine-tuning high-quality output.

CHAPTER 12: INTEGRATING GPT-3/4 WITH YOUR EXISTING CODEBASES AND REAL-WORLD APPLICATIONS.

Combining GPT-3/4 into your current projects and codebases in real-world applications is one of the most effective ways to add project capabilities.

You can easily incorporate OpenAI models, whether working on a web app or desktop application (or any other tech solution) and AI-driven functionalities such as natural language processing, bot capabilities, code generation, etc.

How to Start by Integrating GPT-3/4, sample Scripts to add some spice to your building.

1. Getting OpenAI's API Credentials.

The initial step to achieve, before integrating, is to allow OpenAI API, a very easy process in which you must register for an API key from OpenAI. You can then call the model, e.g. (GPT-3 or GPT-4) using your favorite programming language with that key.

The SDKs are available for official libraries from OpenAI on the most common programming environments available. The libraries openai (Python) or openai-node (JavaScript) gives you a handle to make calls to the model and get the responses you can then wrap into your code.

E.g. for Python, Install OpenAI by pip package:

Pip install openai.

After, you can authorize yourself and start calling the requests to get text output, answer questions, or add built-in AI functionality to your existing app.

2. Choosing the Right Endpoint.

And with the OpenAI API, picking the right model for your purposes becomes important. GPT-3 and GPT-4 have different strengths, making choosing one dependent on how you plan to use your model. GPT-3 is fast and incredibly quick for most doings; GPT -4 delivers more precision and complex understanding — particularly further inquiry or intricate executions.

You can use the text-DaVinci-003 (GPT-3) or GPT-4 endpoints to generate text in your app (depending on whether your actions are relatively light). Be wary of request limits, latency, and the associated costs when choosing between models.

1. Integrate API Calls Into Your Codebase.

Now, we move to adding API calls to your codebase. It can be done by adding GPT-3 / 4 into your app, e.g., in back-end services, front-end user interfaces or serverless functions. For instance, you could send some user input to the API of the chatbot app and give back the AI response to the user.

Example in Python:

```
import openai.

openai.api_key = "your-api-key"

response = openai.Completion.create(

 engine="text-davinci-003", # Or use GPT-4 for higher accuracy.
```

```
prompt="Translate 'Hello' to Spanish,"

max_tokens=60

)

print(response.choices[0].text.strip())
```

Your back-end will feed a prompt in prompts; listen for the model's output in this instance with GPT-3. This can be expanded to include more creative tasks such as creating summaries, writing product descriptions, switching text, or answering customer queries.

4. bind AI with Front-End Components.

It can improve UX as the front end allows AI abilities in a web application. For example, when creating the FAQ section on a website, you can employ GPT-3/4 to generate answers for the user. This would imply that you can have AI dynamically compute answers pertinent to user queries, replacing the static response.

For example, integration of GPT-3/4 into a React app can look like this:

```
import React, { useState } from 'react';
```

```javascript
import axios from 'axios';


const ChatBot = () => {

const [userInput, setUserInput] = useState('');

const [response, setResponse] = useState('');


const handleInputChange = (e) => {

setUserInput(e.target.value);

};


const handleSubmit = async () => {

const result = await axios.post('/api/query', { prompt:
userInput });

setResponse(result.data.reply);

};


return (
```

```jsx
    <div>

     <input

     type="text"

     value={userInput}

     onChange={handleInputChange}

     placeholder="Ask a question"

     />

     <button
onClick={handleSubmit}>Submit</button>

     <p>{response}</p>

    </div>

   );

  };


export default ChatBot;

   •
```

In this example, how you call the front-end an API response that sends user input to GPT-3/4 and fetches AI's response live.

5. Boosting current features with AI.

One of the coolest parts you can do with GPT-3/4 in real-world application integration is its ability to beef up existing features. For example, if your application is already pumping through lots of data, use GPT-3 to summarize, categorize, or analyze.

For example, Task: Users input tasks in the Project management app. You can leverage GPT—3 to assist in producing descriptions or even think of fixing your task list. For example, in an e-commerce app, GPT-3 can help to construct product descriptions, or a client support rep can automate manual replies to provide faster answers.

6. Testing and Scaling your Integration.

Testing is vital when hooking GPT-3/4 into your app. You need to check at what rate the performance is and confirm whether the AI's response should meet the application requirements. This includes testing for edge cases, performing stress to determine if your API can handle many requests and optimizing for performance.

After you are sure that the integration is working, the scaling of the integration is done. Though, like openAI's API, it can handle loads of requests, you need to ensure that your backend services are good at handling the burden of those multiple APIs to prevent user experience degradation.

7. Ensuring Ethical Use/Handling of Data.

When weaving AI into actual living applications, user privacy and ethical thinking should be combined with integration in most classes. Ensure that data sent to OpenAI's servers adheres to your existing privacy policy, and don't send sensitive information out unnecessarily.

Not only do responsible AI-driven applications create value, but they also build a trusting relationship between you and your users.

GPT-3/4 Combined with your old codebase, it will do wonders for your applications; just give them more intelligence and interactivity with your apps. You can use the OpenAI models to create chatbots, improve user interfaces or automate other processes.

Using these AI features well, you can improve the functionality of your app and create more interactive, user-friendly experiences.

CHAPTER 13: CREATE YOUR FIRST AI APP WITH OPENAI'S MODELS.

Understandably, creating an AI app appears to be a difficult endeavor, but with the current toolset and resources, you can easily build one. The app uses OpenAI's robust models, GPT-3 and GPT4, to work with text understanding, generation, etc. If you are building a chatbot, a content writing assistance or an AI customer support app, these models will help you with all of them.

This chapter provides a walk-through on how to create your first AI app with OpenAI's models.

Step 1: Know the Purpose of Your App.

Before you start gobbling up the technical specifics, something should be clear to you — what do you want your app to do? What problem are you solving? Who is your user? The purpose of your app, when defined, will help you deduce when things like OpenAI models should be integrated.

For example, you want a chatbot for your customer service that can answer frequently asked questions and provide some more useful topics. Knowing that upfront will help you focus on the features and data that matter in your app.

Step 2: openai API access.

Sign up to get your API key. The application's API key is used to authenticate requests to enable you interact with the models properly.

Step 3: Choose Your Development Stack.

You must select what kind of tools and tech to develop your app. Models through the OpenAI API can be anything that makes HTTP requests: programming language, Python, JavaScript (Node.js), even serverless functions! For this example, let's assume you are in Python.

Do Install the required Tools:

Python: Your machine should be running Python 3.6 or above.

OpenAI Package for Python: Simply run the

  pip install openai

Step 4: Making Your First API Call.

You need to be able to call OpenAI's models in your AI app, which is its core. We will write a script to do a simple API call and generate the text. That chatbot will take user input and generate a response to it, something like –

import openai.

openai.api_key = "your-api-key"

def ask_bot(question):

  response = openai.Completion.create(

    engine="text-davinci-003", # or gpt-4 for more complex tasks.

    prompt=question,

    max_tokens=150.

)

```
    return response.choices[0].text.strip()

# Test the chatbot

print(ask_bot("What is the capital of France?"))
```

Below is a basic script that queries OpenAI's model and receives its response. max_tokens controls the response length and you input your question in the prompt.

Step 5: Design Your User Interface.

After that, make an interface for users with whom you want to interact with your AI. Solution: Use Python to make a web or mobile app. We will create a basic web app using Flask or Django if you use Python.

Example of a simple Flask-based web interface for creating a bot!

Install Flask:

```
pip install flask
```

Create a simple Flask app (app.py):

```
from flask import Flask, request, render_template.
```

```python
import openai

openai.api_key = "your-api-key"

app = Flask(__name__)

@app.route("/", methods=["GET", "POST"])
def home():
  if request.method == "POST":
    question = request.form["question"]

    answer = ask_bot(question)

    return render_template("index.html",
answer=answer)

  return render_template("index.html")

def ask_bot(question):
  response = openai.Completion.create(
    engine="text-davinci-003",

    prompt=question,

    max_tokens=150
  )
```

```python
    return response.choices[0].text.strip()

if __name__ == "__main__":

    app.run(debug=True)
```

Create an index.html file for the user interface:

```html
<!DOCTYPE html>

<html>

<head>

  <title>Chat with AI</title>

</head>

<body>

  <h1>Ask the AI anything!</h1>

  <form method="POST">

    <input type="text" name="question"
placeholder="Ask a question" required>

    <button type="submit">Ask</button>

  </form>
```

```
{% if answer %}

  <h2>Answer: {{ answer }}</h2>

  {% endif %}

</body>

</html>
```

You can type a question in a text box, click submit, and view the AI response within this Flask app. We discuss the backend code that uses OpenAI's API to get a response, which is then shown on a webpage.

Step 6: Test & Refine Your App.

After implementing functionality, You must test and iterate on your app now. This is what you should be wary of:

Is the interface easy to use?

Do the responses from the AI make sense and is it correct?

Error Handling: Ensure you gracefully handle errors in your app, including errors with invalid API keys, network issues or the AI not returning what's expected.

Performance: Think about how to do many API calls efficiently if you need your app to scale

Step 7: Deploy Your App

Once your app is local, it is time to deploy it; for the web, you can use services such as Heroku, AWS, or Google Cloud to deploy your app. For mobile, all in app stores like Google Play or Apple Appstore and deploy your app. Ensure you adequately test everything in the deployment environment before rolling out the app to your users.

Step 8: iterate and improve

AI in the app is only at the start. You can keep improving the app with

• Improve response quality using prompts hard-fine-tuner.

• Adding in more features (add speech recognition & other APIs)

• Gathering the user feedback and improving the user experience.

Building an AI app in your OpenAI model sounds very cool and a cool ride. By doing the above, you can build a relevant, intelligent application that adds user value. Unlimited possibilities are possible with the adaptability and power of OpenAI models, whether you are building a chatbot, assistant, bots, or essentially anything else powered by AI.

CONCLUSION.

As we conclude this adventure of exploring the OpenAI Playground, we can understand that we have just scratched the surface of the infinite power held by OpenAI models.

From the time you step into the Playground, you are no longer in dialogue with a tool but rather the playground of infinite creativity, solving and innovating.

Suppose you are creating basic applications and wish to experiment with text generation or get into the interesting specifics of AI programming. In that case, Playground is your medium for shaping, sculpting, and editing ideas in a way that never felt easier.

OpenAI playground is different and magical because it is easy to use and implement. That was where AI once lived, in the intellectual high-tech laboratories or exotic research institutions.

The Playground is an opportunity for just about anybody who is far from an experienced developer, to give it a test run with cutting-edge models such as GPT-3, GPT-4, and Codex.

All it needs is an unsticky mind and you won't let curiosity die. This is a realm where people of all types can harness the capabilities of artificial intelligence, taking part in the great AI revolution already happening.

The most awe-inspiring thing about the Playground is that you can do much with it. With just writing prompts, the ideas are endless: creative writing, code, chatbots, educational applications, you name it!

The real trick is how they translate those abstractions to real-world applications for different use cases. For example, this could be the simplest (and yet hardest) thing in which you ask a question and, in return, a story, a line from the code, a solution or even a whole idea of a new product, all because the models are so adaptable.

But it is not only the technology. Well, that happens with us and this technology. The Playground forces us to be ethical, thoughtful, and careful when dealing with

AI. From the previous chapters on fairness and bias, it suffices to say that responsible AI development is important.

The OpenAI models are huge, but with talents, these powers come with a duty to use ethically and for the benefit of all. We, the creators, developers and users of this technology, are its collective stewards. This is why establishing fairness, transparency and inclusivity in the models we build and release is crucial to creating a better tomorrow.

What is equally mind-blowing is that Playground paves the way for creativity. Using AI, we can sketch out new worlds, new solution spaces and uncharted areas of expression. Picture GPT-4 writing poetry (dialog between characters to compose a narrative progression on the fly).

It is no longer for artists, authors, or coders; the things that were once within the boundaries are no longer. Art, Literature and education are possibilities that are endless in business. OpenAI has knocked down the gates to a creative frontier where human creativity will coexist and collaborate with machines to rewrite the possible.

If you are a developer and you want similar projects that you can make real, Playground is the space to experiment and test ideas before they are in full form. With access to these cutting-edge models (e.g., Codex), users can start writing and testing code or even building applications/automating processes through the conduit.

Playground, with its live feedback and iterations, is the best place to practice your skills if you are working on your first AI app or debugging ancient code. The OpenAI Playground is what truly makes this place so special through the potential that it invokes. It is an incubation ground to nurture your ideas, hone them, and grow your understanding of AI in one place.

Every experiment, every new prompt, every rework gets you one step closer to owning this technology and taking full advantage of what it can do. Whether playing with the Playground for fun, learning, or business, you enable people to contribute something far greater — shaping the future.

In virtually all sectors of life, including healthcare, finance, media, and education, the reality of AI is already being experienced. However, what makes AI truly revolutionary is not being able to automate tasks or amplify human performance.

Its true strength is in the spark that it ignites human creativity and solves problems we have never even imagined to explore new frontiers. Playground is the way to this future, and anyone, anywhere, can start their adventure in AI.

Ultimately, Exploring the OpenAI Playground is not just a tutorial for using AI models. It is an offer to enter new dimensions of innovation, creativity and potential. Regardless of the complexity of an app you are building, a masterpiece of art you are creating or your discovery of how (and how not) AI can enliven every aspect of life around us.

The Playground gives you access to powerful means of production and free opportunities to turn your ideas into physical artifacts. AI is a big gleam in our future, and you hold the key to that future in your hands while using OpenAI Playground, so don't sit back and watch what happens.

Series

"Smarter Strategies for Modern Business"

Exploring the Open AI Playground: Unleasing Creativity with AI

"Social Media Influence."

Increasing your Social Media Influence on Facebook.
Increasing your Social Media Influence on YouTube.
Increasing your Social Media Influence on Instagram.
Increasing your Social Media Influence on TikTok.
Increasing your Social Media Influence on Reddit.
Increasing your Social Media Influence on Pinterest.
Increasing your Social Media Influence on Twitter.
Increasing your Social Media Influence on LinkedIn.

Please check out Amazon for more books in this collection.

Author Bio

Aaron is passionate about reading and learning how to maximize profitability on social media. Inspired by her knowledge and enthusiasm, she decided to share her insights through writing. This book is just the beginning—more titles are coming in this collection! Be sure to follow her on Amazon to stay updated on future releases.

Thank you for your purchase! Your support truly means the world to me, and I deeply appreciate you as a valued reader. God Bless You.

Aaron Cockman.

ISBN 9798319262691

90000